MONSTER

P H O N I C S

Short Vowels
For Grades K–1

By Vicky Shiotsu

Illustrated by Lucy Helle

LOWELL HOUSE JUVENILE

LOS ANGELES

NTC/Contemporary Publishing Group

Reviewed and endorsed by Dr. Peg Hughes, Assistant Professor at California State University, Fullerton, School of Human Development and Community Service, Education Division

About the Author

Vicky Shiotsu graduated from the University of British Columbia with a Bachelor's degree in Education and taught elementary school at various grade levels for eight years. She has also worked as a tutor to Japanese students, a teacher at a reading center, and as an editor/writer for an educational publishing company.

Published by Lowell House
A division of NTC/Contemporary Publishing Group, Inc.
4255 West Touhy Avenue, Lincolnwood (Chicago), Illinois 60646-1975 U.S.A.

Managing Director and Publisher: Jack Artenstein
Director of Publishing Services: Rena Copperman
Editorial Director: Brenda Pope-Ostrow
Director of Art Production: Bret Perry
Editor: Linda Gorman
Designer: Carolyn Wendt
Color Artist: Kristi Mathias

Series logo created by Jack Keely

Lowell House books can be purchased at special discounts when ordered in bulk for premiums and special sales. Please contact Customer Service at:
NTC/Contemporary Publishing Group
4255 West Touhy Avenue
Lincolnwood, IL 60646-1975
1-800-323-4900

Printed in Hong Kong by Imago

ISBN: 0-7373-0143-0

10 9 8 7 6 5 4 3 2 1

Note to Parents

Monster Phonics is a wonderful learning tool that will help your child build a strong foundation in phonics. A community of lovable monsters present and teach the activities in this workbook, helping your child develop a knowledge of short vowels. The appealing activities also encourage listening and reading comprehension, analytical thinking, and problem solving. What a great way to instill a love of learning!

The activities in this book offer your child opportunities to practice a wide range of skills. Activities include distinguishing the sounds of short vowels, reading and writing words with short vowels, finding hidden pictures, completing mazes, and more! It is best that your child complete the activities in the order that they are presented, since some of the pages build on skills practiced earlier in the book.

As your child works through the pages, give plenty of praise and encouragement. Each activity is designed to ensure success and stimulate interest. If your child likes to work independently, let him or her do so. If your child prefers you to read the sentences aloud, then by all means do that. After each activity is done, you and your child can turn to the back of the book to check the answers. Later, when all the pages have been completed, present your child with the colorful award provided on the last page of the book.

Learning is an exciting and rewarding experience. Whether your child is a phonics marvel or is just becoming aware of the relationship between letters and sounds, he or she will benefit from each motivating activity in the **Monster Phonics** series! You will find that as your child masters the various skills presented in these activity books, he or she will develop and display the traits of a confident, enthusiastic learner.

SHORT VOWEL CHART
Beginning Sounds

Point to each vowel. Say its name. Then say the name of each picture. Listen to the beginning sound.

a

ant

e

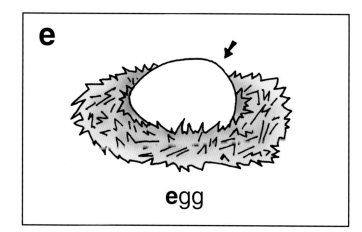

egg

i

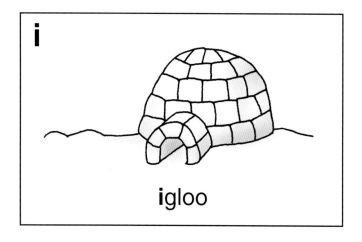

igloo

o

octopus

u

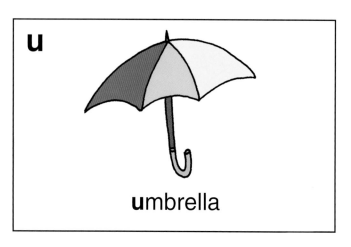

umbrella

Introduction to short vowels

SHORT VOWEL CHART
Middle Sounds

Point to each vowel. Say its name. Then say the name of each picture. Listen to the middle sound.

a

hat

e

bed

i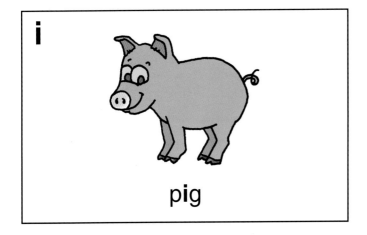

pig

o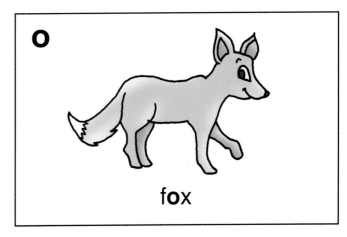

fox

u

duck

ANDY'S PICTURES

Help Andy label his pictures by tracing the words. Then say the words aloud. Listen to the sound that the **a** makes.

apple

ant

add

ax

*Recognizing the short **a** sound*

IN THE ATTIC

These pictures have short **a** in their names.

mat   rat   lamp   bat   mask

Find them in Andy's attic. Color them yellow. Then color the rest of the picture any way you like.

*Identifying words that have short **a***

AN AMAZING MACHINE

Andy made an amazing machine. It pops out things that have a short **a** sound! Write the missing **a** for each word below. Then say the words aloud.

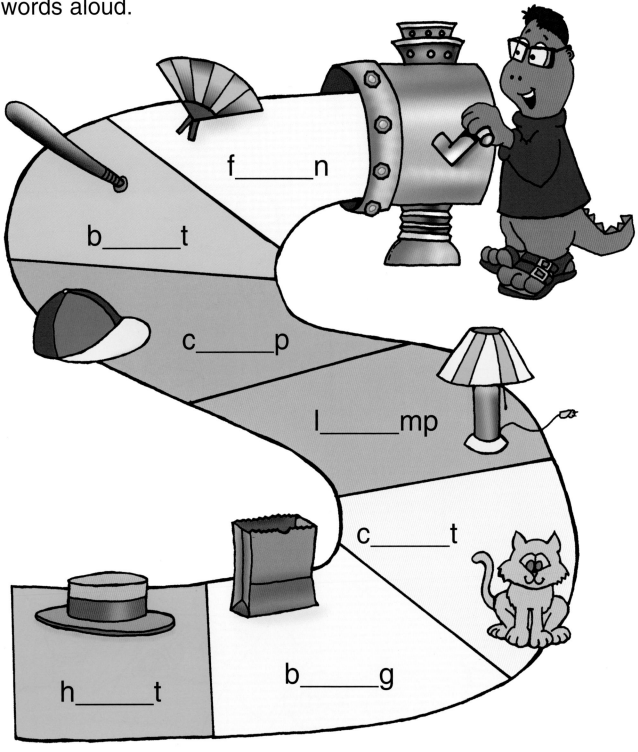

f_____n

b_____t

c_____p

l_____mp

c_____t

h_____t

b_____g

Completing words, reading words with short a

A FUNNY COSTUME

Look at Andy's funny costume! Draw a line from each word to its matching picture.

hat

mask

bag

ant

fan

bat

pants

cat

IN ELMO'S ROOM

Here are some things that are in Elmo's room. Label them by tracing the words. Then say the words aloud. Listen to the sound that the **e** makes.

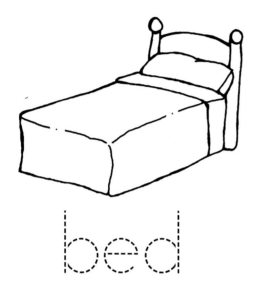

bed

pen

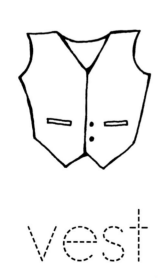

vest

desk

Recognizing the short e sound

FUN ON A SLED

Help the monsters ride their sled down the hill. Write **e** on the lines to complete the words. Then say the words aloud.

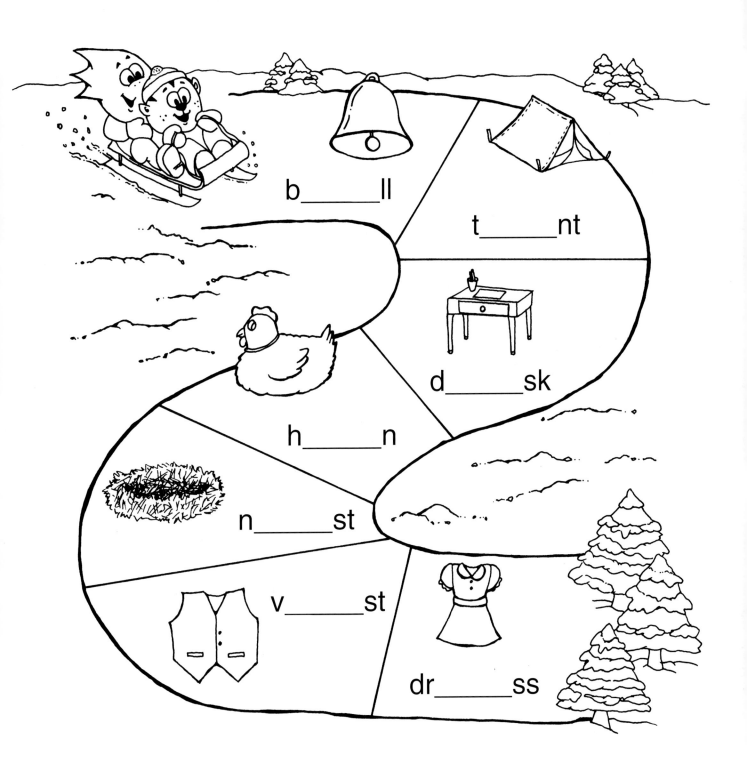

b_____ll

t_____nt

d_____sk

h_____n

n_____st

v_____st

dr_____ss

ELMO'S WORDS

Elmo wrote words that have short **e**. Draw a line from each word to its picture.

pen

net

web

bell

hen

tent

vest

desk

*Reading words with short **e***

SCHOOLTIME

Help Andy and Elmo do their homework. Label the pictures. Write **a** or **e** on the lines to complete each word.

f_____n

_____gg

_____x

c_____t

t_____nt

l_____mp

b_____ll

h_____t

h_____n

b_____t

m_____sk

sl_____d

*Distinguishing short **a** and short **e***

IZZY'S GIFTS

Look at Izzy's birthday gifts! Help her label them by tracing the words. Then say the words aloud. Listen to the sound that the **i** makes.

ring

mitt

pig

dish

*Recognizing the short **i** sound*

A BIG SHIP

Look at the pictures on the ship's sails. Color the ones that have short **i** in their names.

*Identifying words that have short **i***

MAKE A WISH

The monsters are at a wishing well. Find out what each one is hoping to get. Write **i** on the lines to complete each word. Then say the words aloud.

r_____ng

m_____tt

p_____g

d_____sh

f_____sh

w_____g

Completing words, reading words with short i

IZZY'S TRIP

Izzy is taking a trip to the North Pole. Help her get to her friend's igloo. Circle the correct word for each picture on the path.

fix   six

pin   tin

hill   pill

dish   fish

gift   lift

big   pig

wing   ring

king   sing

WHO'S HIDING?

Find out who's hiding below. If a space has a picture of a short **a** word, color it blue. If a space has a picture of a short **i** word, color it red.

Circle who you found.   cat   fish

*Distinguishing short **a** and short **i***

A PRETTY QUILT

Elmo and Izzy need to finish their quilt. Circle the correct word for each picture. Then color the quilt any way you like.

tip
ten

pen
pig

bed
bit

pig
pen

bell
bill

lid
leg

tent
tint

pin
pet

hit
hen

*Distinguishing short **e** and short **i***

19

IN THE WOODS

Help the monsters get to their tents. Write the words for the pictures on the path. Use the words on the hill on the next page.

Review of short vowels a, e, i

cap   pen   gift

bat   web   pig

van   bed   bib

lamp   dress   ring

*Review of short vowels **a, e, i***

OLIVE'S BOX

What things are in Olive's box? Find out by tracing the words below. Then say the words aloud. Listen to the sound that the **o** makes.

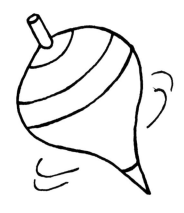

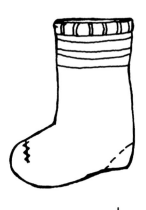

Recognizing the short o sound

OLIVE'S DOLL

Olive wants to find her doll. Make a path for her. Color the pictures that have short **o** in their names.

MONSTER HOP

Help Olive and her friend Otto hop across the pond. Write the missing **o** for each word. Then say the words aloud.

l_____g

t_____p

b_____x

f_____x

m_____p

d_____g

r_____ck

Completing words, reading words with short **o**

AT THE POND

Look at the pictures on the lily pads. Write the word for each picture. Use the words on the log.

pot   box   dog   lock
fox   top   doll   sock

SORT THE PAPERS

Andy and Olive dropped their homework. Help them pick up their papers. First write **a** or **o** to complete the words below. Then draw lines from the short **a** words to Andy. Draw lines from the short **o** words to Olive.

fr_____g

r_____t

m_____p

l_____mp

r_____ck

p_____t

c_____p

f_____n

*Distinguishing short **a** and short **o***

TIME TO STUDY

Find four things in the picture that have short **e** in their names. Color them red. Find four things that have short **o** in their names. Color them blue.

*Distinguishing short **e** and short **o***

A YARD SALE

Label all the things
that are for sale.
Use the words on
the sign.

Things for Sale

bib	doll	wig
mop	pot	lock
dish	ring	clock

28

RHYME TIME

Draw pictures for the rhyming words below.

sad dad

wet pet

big pig

hot pot

COLORFUL BALLOONS

Look at the pictures on the balloons. Say their names and listen to the vowel sounds. Then use the code to color the balloons.

Code

short **a** — blue   short **i** — yellow

short **e** — red   short **o** — green

*Review of short vowels **a, e, i, o***

TIME FOR BED

Read the words. Circle the correct word for each picture.

bill
bell

hat
hit

net
not

sock
sick

wag
wig

dash
dish

lad
lid

sack
sock

fox
fix

bag
big

map
mop

tint
tent

Review of short vowels a, e, i, o

UG'S PUPPETS

Ug collects puppets. Some of his puppets are shown below. Label them by tracing the words. Then say the words aloud. Listen to the sound that the **u** makes.

bug

pup

cub

duck

*Recognizing the short **u** sound*

A BUS RIDE

The monsters are riding a bus to school. Help them get there on time. Write the missing **u** for the words below. Then say the words aloud.

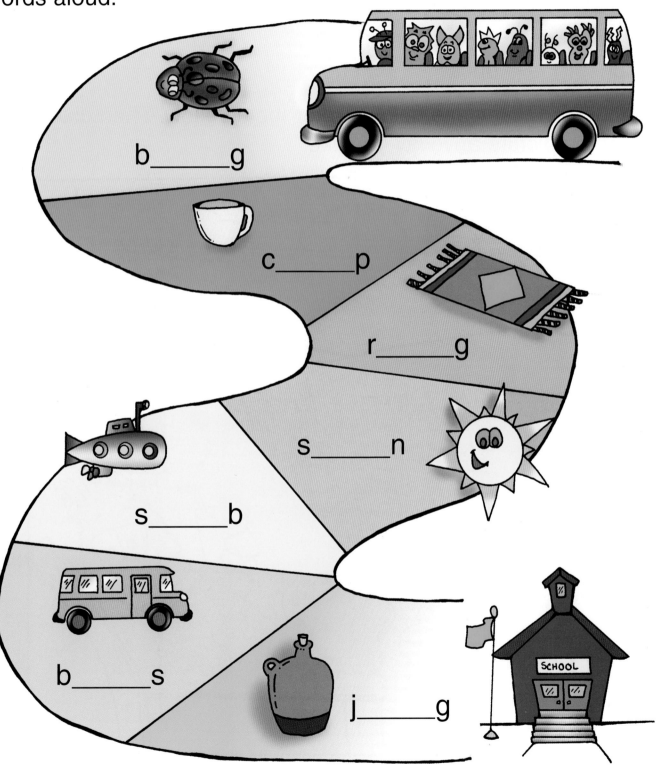

b____g

c____p

r____g

s____n

s____b

b____s

j____g

FUN IN THE SUN

These pictures have short **u** in their names.

sun   duck   cup   jug   hut

Find them in the scene below. Color them yellow. Then color the rest of the picture any way you like.

Identifying words that have short u

SPLISH, SPLASH

Label the pictures in the puddle. Use the words on the umbrella.

nut   jug   duck   bug

hut   mug   truck   tub

MONSTER ACTIONS

Write **a** or **u** on the lines to complete each word. Then read the sentences.

Andy can r_____n.

Elmo can j_____mp.

Izzy can c_____tch.

Olive can cl_____p.

Ug can c_____t.

The monsters can _____dd.

*Distinguishing short **a** and short **u***

COLLECTING STUFF

Elmo and Ug are collecting all kinds of stuff. Elmo is collecting things that have a short **e** sound in their names. Ug is collecting things that have a short **u** sound. Draw a line from each object to the correct box.

*Distinguishing short **e** and short **u***

PICNIC FUN

Help Izzy and Ug get to the picnic basket. Circle the correct word for each picture on the path.

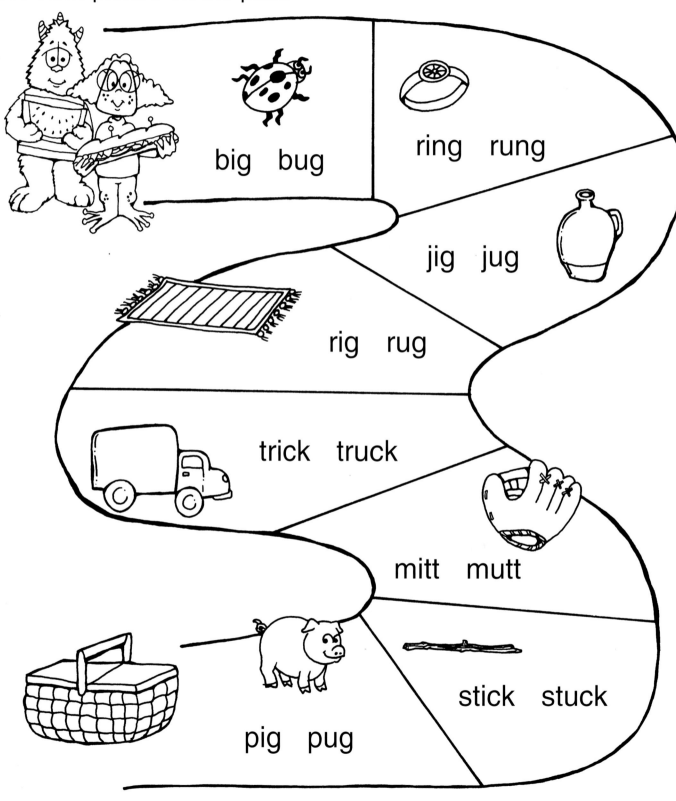

big   bug

ring   rung

jig   jug

rig   rug

trick   truck

mitt   mutt

stick   stuck

pig   pug

*Distinguishing short **i** and short **u***

AT THE DUCK POND

Olive and Ug want to feed the ducks. Make a path to the pond for them. Write **o** or **u** on the lines to complete each word.

l___g

r___ck

c___p

d___t

b___s

s___n

s___ck

b___g

n___t

dr___m

b___x

ANIMAL SNAPSHOTS

The monsters took pictures of
some animals. Label the pictures.
Write **a, e, i, o,** or **u** on the lines.

p_____g

c_____t

b_____t

h_____n

_____nt

f_____sh

d_____g

fr_____g

d_____ck

Distinguishing short vowels

AT THE TOY SHOP

Look at the vowel at the beginning of each row. Then name the toys in the row. Circle the toys that have the matching vowel sound.

Distinguishing short vowels

MONSTER GALLERY

Read the words. Draw pictures to match.

a big bus

six bugs

a wet doll

a hot sun

ten rocks

Reading words with short vowels

RIDDLE TIME

Read the riddles. Write the answers. Use the words at the bottom of the page.

1. This has six legs. _____

2. This can spin fast. _____

3. This can ring and ring. _____

4. This is a soft pet. _____

5. This is a man. _____

6. This is very hot. _____

sun

bell

cat

king

top

bug

PET SHOP GAME

This is a game for two players. Ask a parent or a friend to play with you. You will need one coin and two markers.

Directions

1. Each player places a marker on the space marked **Start**.

2. Take turns flipping the coin and moving your marker along the game board. If the coin lands heads up, move one space. If it lands tails up, move two spaces.

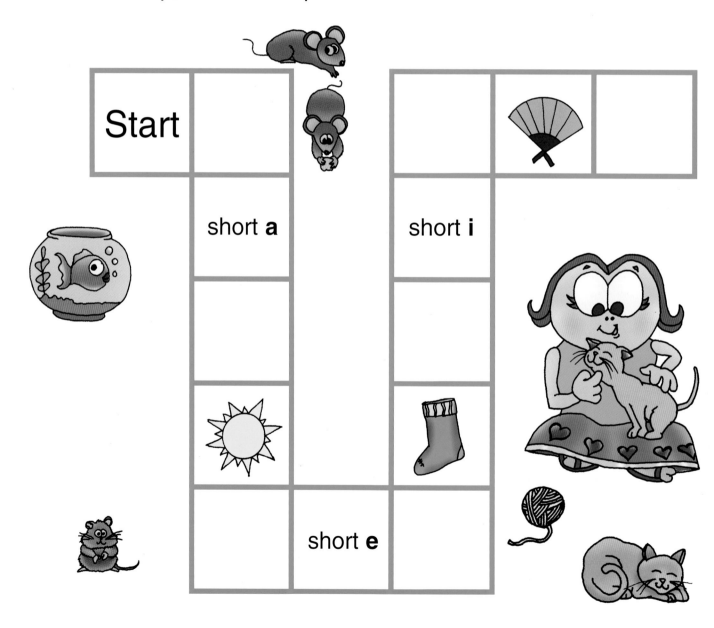

44

Review of short vowels

3. If a player lands on a short vowel, he or she says a word that has that sound and moves an extra space forward.

4. If a player lands on a picture, he or she names it and tells which short vowel is in the word. Then the player moves an extra space forward.

5. The first player to reach the puppies in the pet shop wins.

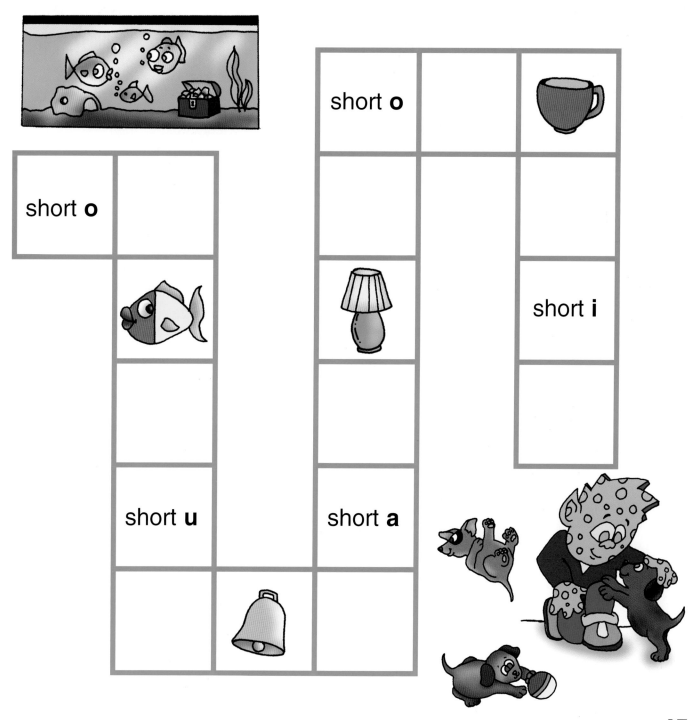

Answers

Page 6
These words should be traced:
apple, ant, add, ax.

Page 7

Page 8
These words should be completed: fan, bat, cap, lamp, cat, bag, hat.

Page 9

Page 10
These words should be traced:
bed, pen, vest, desk.

Page 11
These words should be completed: bell, tent, desk, hen, nest, vest, dress.

Page 12
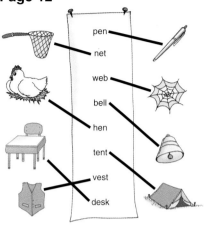

Page 13
fan   **e**gg   **a**x
cat   tent   lamp
b**e**ll   hat   h**e**n
b**a**t   m**a**sk   sl**e**d

Page 14
These words should be traced:
ring, mitt, pig, dish.

Page 15
The sails with these pictures should be colored: 6 (six), ring, pin, fish, bib.

Page 16
These words should be completed: ring, pig, fish, wig, dish, mitt.

Page 17
These words should be circled:
six, pin, hill, pig, gift, fish, ring, king.

Page 18
These short **a** objects should be colored blue: fan, ax, hat, bag, can, lamp, cap, bat.
These short **i** objects should be colored red: pin, bib, 6 (six), pig, wig, mitt, ring.

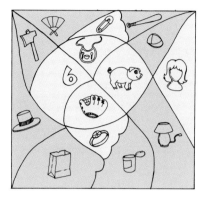

A fish is hidden in the picture.

Page 19
These words should be circled:
ten   pig   bed
pen   bell   lid
tent   pin   hen

Pages 20–21
These words should be written on the path in the following order:
bat, web, pig, cap, gift, bed, van, bib, pen, dress, lamp, ring.

Page 22
These words should be traced:
top, sock, doll, clock.

Page 23
These pictures should be shaded:
mop, box, log, sock, top, lock, block, doll.

Page 24

These words should be completed: log, top, box, mop, fox, dog, rock.

Page 25

Page 26

Lines should be drawn from these words to Andy: rat, lamp, cap, fan. Lines should be drawn from these words to Olive: frog, mop, rock, pot.

Page 27

These items should be colored red: web, pen, desk, bed. These items should be colored blue: clock, box, doll, sock.

Page 28

wig	mop	bib
ring	pot	dish
lock	doll	clock

Page 29

Pictures should be drawn to match the four rhyming phrases.

Page 30

blue short **a** words: fan, cap, can
red short **e** words: bell, bed
yellow short **i** words: fish, pin, pig, mitt
green short **o** words: box, sock, log

Page 31

These words should be circled:

bell	hat	net
sock	wig	dish
lid	sack	fox
bag	mop	tent

Page 32

These words should be traced: bug, pup, cub, duck.

Page 33

These words should be completed: bug, cup, rug, sun, sub, bus, jug.

Page 34

Page 35

Page 36

Andy can r**u**n.
Elmo can j**u**mp.
Izzy can c**a**tch.
Olive can cl**a**p.
Ug can c**u**t.
The monsters can **a**dd.

Page 37

Lines should be drawn from these pictures to the short **e** box: bell, net, pen, egg.
Lines should be drawn from these pictures to the short **u** box: cup, rug, duck, drum.

Page 38

These words should be circled: bug, ring, jug, rug, truck, mitt, stick, pig.

Page 39

l**o**g	r**o**ck	cup
dot	bus	sun
sock	bug	nut
drum	b**o**x	

Page 40

p**i**g	cat	bat
hen	ant	fish
dog	fr**o**g	d**u**ck

Page 41

These toys should be circled:
short **a**: bat, fan
short **e**: bell, net
short **i**: ring, mitt
short **o**: top, doll
short **u**: duck, sub

Page 42

Pictures should be drawn to match the five phrases.

Page 43

1. bug
2. top
3. bell
4. cat
5. king
6. sun

Pages 44–45

The vowels in the names of the pictures on the game board are as follows:

sun – u	bell – e
sock – o	lamp – a
fan – a	cup – u
fish – i